The Educator's Diet
TEACHING WITH 21ST CENTURY RECIPES

© 2015 by Carol Woodard. All rights reserved.

Printed in the United States of America
ISBN-13: 978-1517562960
ISBN-10: 1517562961

Better today because of…

SHELTON OGLE
the one who pushed me to achieve more

JANET FISHER
the one who inspired me to be a better educator

MARK, JILL & ANGIE
the ones who are my heart & soul

Recipes Inside

APPETIZER
STIMULATING YOUR DESIRE TO EAT

    Introducing the Diet   9

SOUP & SALAD
CLASSROOM TOOLS USED IN A HEALTHY WAY

1. Power Point   13
2. Whiteboards and Flipcharts   15
3. Tablets   17
4. Props   19

MAIN COURSE
THE MEAT – CAROLISMS

5. Keep learning. Students make the best educators.   23
6. Great coaches know why their players joined the team.   25
7. Make them curious … and they will come.   27
8. Adapt to the student. Don't make them adapt to you.   29
9. Embrace change. Always.   31
10. Teach your students, but work your room.   35
11. Don't teach to the test. Teach for understanding   37
12. Allow your students to make mistakes.   39
13. Celebrate the success of your students.   41
14. Cheer them on! Be a dream maker, not a dream stealer.   43

DESSERT
SWEET TIPS TO SATISFY YOU

15. What If Your Student Is Older Than You?	49
16. The Importance of Thank You	51
17. Teaching to the Auditory Learner	53
18. Cell Phones: The #1 Battle You'll Never Win	55
19. Dealing With the Know-It-All	58
20. Winning the Introvert	60

COFFEE
FINISHERS TO TAKE YOU TO THE NEXT LEVEL

21. Are You the Reason Your Students are Late?	65
22. How Do You Serve Your Mashed Potatoes?	67
23. Grading 101	69
24. Setting Up Your Classroom to Make You – Not Break You	71
25. Are You Personally Grounded?	73
26. When Your Student Keeps Failing	75
27. Is Quitting Your Job the Answer?	77

TAKEOUT
ACTIVITIES TO BRING TO CLASS

28. Icebreakers	83
29. Build Them Up	86
30. Team Building	88

PERSONAL REFLECTIONS   91

APPETIZER
Stimulating Your Desire to Eat

Introducing the Diet

A diet means change—breaking old habits, finding a healthy balance to better yourself and giving up things that aren't good for you. It's interesting how diets have developed over the years. One guru says to eat only meat and then science determines that's probably not the best idea.

Have you noticed how in the past few years "gluten" is the hot word and everyone's trying to cut it out of his or her diet. As we learn more, live longer and dive into the science of our bodies, we will find diets that work and others that don't.

That's exactly how I feel about teaching. Education is my passion. It's at the core of who I am and I love developing new methods that actually work. Whether you want to admit it or not, our students are different than they were ten years ago. Our old tricks don't necessarily work on these narcissistic, social media obsessed, tech-savvy kids that can't concentrate for more than eight seconds.

I'm going to push you. I want you to be better. I want you to embrace change and get out of your comfort zone. Change is the new black and I'm here to impart my best-kept secrets from nearly 20 years as an educator. This book will address a variety of topics that cover a span of issues teachers deal with on a regular basis.

These recipes will require ingredients that you already have. You already possess the skills to be a life-changing teacher—I'm just going to help you find a way to make the perfect dish. Some of these will be challenging. Others you might already be doing. I encourage you to take time to examine yourself and review your effectiveness as an educator.

Let's change lives together, embrace the new and never underestimate the power of an educator!

SOUP & SALAD
Classroom Tools Used in a Healthy Way

1
Power Point

Let me start by saying this: I am not a graphic designer, I am not a tech guru and I am not someone who custom-designs Power Point presentations for a living. I am a teacher—a communicator.

If you are someone who relies on Power Point to teach, then I strongly suggest you focus on developing your in-person presence. (There are some great chapters in this book that will help you do just that!) There will be times when technology fails or your slides become too mundane for students. That is why it's important to never rely solely on your slides to get you through a class.

That being said, Power Point can be a very effective tool in the classroom if used correctly. My tips come solely from experience using Power Point as a teacher. Power Point can be used in a variety of ways and in a variety of industries—but as an educator, there are specifics you need to know before developing your slides.

1. Make your presentation in 16:9 instead of 4:3. Wide screen looks sharper and most videos you import will be in 16:9.
2. Stay consistent with your template and overall design.
3. Watch your colors. For example, red words on a black background are hard to read.
4. Use pictures and video to tell your story — very few words! My opinion is not to have more than 30% of the slide with words on it. When there are too many words, students start reading the slides instead of listening to you.
5. When adding photos, add "soft edges" to the picture in settings

so that it blends better. Often times pictures look poorly thrown on.

6. Use smooth transitions that aren't too distracting. There's nothing worse than words bouncing all over the place as they enter the screen.

7. When adding video, do not import from YouTube or add a link to an online source. Internet might fail you or maybe that specific video has been taken off YouTube by the time you click it. Always upload an actual video file from the computer you are using Power Point on.

8. Connect your presentations. Whether it's by the overall design, a consistent hashtag at the bottom or a recap of the past presentation—your lessons need to feel cohesive.

9. Double-check for errors. I know this seems obvious, but a tiny mistake on your Power Point is distracting to students. They become fixated on it and can't pay attention to you.

10. Invest in your own clicker. Your clicker needs to feel like your right hand and you should be smooth with moving from slide to slide.

11. Know your content. Power Point presentations are not replacing you—they're enhancing you! You should know your next slide before even advancing to it.

12. Practice, practice, practice. From walking your classroom to making sure your transitions work—practice using your PPT.

There are other great tools on the market that are similar to Power Point that might enhance your presentations even more (like Prezi). When in doubt, head over to YouYube to watch tutorials on how to develop your slides. Sometimes we get so caught up in putting time and effort into our Power Point presentations that we forget to work on developing our teaching skills. I've been there. We all have. Remember—you have the power to make a difference and present information that could change someone's life.

2
Whiteboards and Flipcharts

I love using whiteboards and flipcharts in the classroom, but there is a time and place for using these. The main difference between these tools and something like Power Point is that whiteboards and flipcharts encourage participation and collaboration. You can't change a point or add someone's idea to a slide as you're presenting it, but you can add it to a whiteboard.

If you're having open dialog and you want group input, using a whiteboard or flipchart in your classroom immediately creates conversation. There's something about a student's idea being added to a board that excites them.

When using whiteboards and flipcharts in the classroom:

1. Make sure the board is clean. You can't keep using an eraser over and over again. You need a spray cleaner on it or use a wet rag. Writing on top of a dirty or foggy board is worse than not writing at all.

2. Test your markers before class starts and throw out the bad ones.

3. Test your markers to know which are skinny, fat, etc. Depending on how much you're writing, this is important to know.

4. Test your markers on a whiteboard. Some are squeaky! You want to make sure your markers don't become a distraction in the middle of a great class discussion.

5. Prep your flipchart. Sometimes having facts and figures written lightly in pencil at the top will remind you of a great point to

make while you're teaching. Adding pictures ahead of time to the chart will make for pleasant surprises when you flip the page.

6. If your flipchart has a sticky back and you're planning on peeling and sticking it on the wall—make sure it actually sticks! Sometimes I get a defective pad and then it slides off my walls in the middle of class, causing a giant distraction.

7. Always print—never cursive write.

8. Start writing at the top of a flipchart and go down (would you believe most people start near the middle?!).

9. Unless the front row is set back a good distance from your flipchart, don't use the bottom third of the paper. Every eye needs to see every word.

10. Keep permanent markers away from your whiteboards. We've all been there. We've all felt this humiliation.

This is also a great opportunity for you to choose a student to do the writing while you walk your classroom. I talk about it later in this book, but often times older students or introverts want a role in the classroom, but you're not sure how to include them. This is the perfect way to make them feel important.

You should also be sure to include everyone's thoughts and opinions throughout the discussion on the whiteboard or flipchart. Even if a student gives an answer that might not be as relevant, find a way to tweak their response and repeat it back to them for verification. Like, *"Yes, great thought! So you mean ..."*

Picking and choosing the best responses to write down is a quick way to lose respect and lessen the likelihood of class participation in the future.

3
Tablets

Tablets bring a new experience to the classroom and since its inception only a few years ago, I've seen it transform education. I'm not the most tech-savvy person, but as an embracer of change I knew I needed to get on the bus or I'd be left behind.

Remember: technology isn't technology if it's always been around. A light bulb isn't technology to you and me, but to our great grandparents it was. Tablets are technology to you and me because we didn't always have them, but they aren't to Generation Z because they don't know life without them. Turn on the light bulb and get on board!

When using tablets in the classroom:

1. Don't stress yourself out. You won't know how to use every function or app … and that's OK!
2. Validate your students by thanking them if they show you something you didn't already know. Allow them to teach you. Don't get defensive or act like you already knew it.
3. Take a free class at Apple or go on YouTube to watch tutorials. If you don't know how to tie your shoelace, you better learn. The same goes for tablets.
4. Your students should have "charging homework" every night. Be sure they come to class with full batteries on their tablets.
5. Be patient with older students who will be out of their comfort zone. You can't cater your class to the majority. It's your job to teach to every person … and some require more patience than others.

6. Have your students capture important moments on video. Perhaps it's a live demonstration or an important part of a lecture. Allow your class to take pictures and video.
7. Encourage your students to share daily life at school on their social media posts. Create a hashtag specific for your class that students can add to their posts.
8. Have students check your facts or find videos and pictures that are relevant to your class topic.
9. Take advantage of apps for surveys and teaching tools.
10. Transition from handouts into documents made available on their tablets. You can easily share pdfs for them to store on their tablets.

Many schools give students tablets or the opportunity to purchase them. Don't create classroom activities with tablets unless this is the case.

However, I do have a chapter on incorporating cell phones into the classroom. Many of those same points could be used here. Practically every student should, at the very least, have a cell phone. Allowing students to utilize tools they're already comfortable with will make learning fun for them.

It's not up to you to decide how your students learn. It's up to you to adapt your lesson plans to teach them in the most effective way—even if that means we have to be a little uncomfortable!

4
Props

Call me cheesy, but I love a good prop! Sometimes the best way to bring a story or a lesson to life is to illustrate it with props. Why else do you think "Show and Tell" was such a highlight in elementary school? The "tell" isn't always enough. There is something about pulling out an item from a bag of tricks that excites an audience. It breaks up the mundane routine and is a perfect connector!

When using props in the classroom:

- **Put thought into it ahead of time.** Don't look around your living room the night before class to try to find something that might work into your lesson plan. Look on Pinterest, brainstorm with colleagues and put thought into the props you use.

- **Use them as a teaser.** Give your students a reason to be at school tomorrow! End your class with a prop teaser. They'll be intrigued and wonder how it relates to tomorrow's class.

- **Have it set up in your classroom.** Whether you're teaching anatomy and have a skeleton next to you or a typewriter to teach the evolution of technology—having props pre-set in the room before your students walk in is a great way to get them curious and involved.

- **You don't have to be elaborate.** Maybe you're teaching on a decade so you bring in an item or piece of clothing from that era. Whatever props you decide to include, you don't have to go overboard. They don't have to be expensive or over-the-top.

MAKE THE RECIPE YOUR OWN!

Soup & Salad: Classroom Tools
TAKEAWAYS

Ouch! Areas that stepped on my toes

_____

_____

_____

_____

Something new I learned that I didn't know before

_____

_____

_____

_____

Things I will change immediately (because change is the new black!)

_____

_____

_____

_____

MAIN COURSE
The Meat – Carolisms

5
Carolism #1
Keep learning. Students make the best educators.

Next time it rains, put a bucket outside and collect the water. Check back every so often and you'll find that the water doesn't quite look like water anymore. In fact, it's no longer transparent. It starts to pollute itself and collect bugs and debris. That's what happens to teachers when they stop learning. They get stale.

When you walk into into a classroom, the students need to see your excitement. When you really look at it, teaching is unlike any other job out there. If you work in an office, you might have an hour to yourself before a late-morning meeting—a chance to collect your thoughts, read your emails and wake up. Teachers are "on" immediately. When those students walk in the door, it's up to you to teach, entertain and answer questions.

I meet with educators on a regular basis. Sometimes I'm just an ear to hear personal venting, and that's OK, but many times I'm privileged to get a room full of eager students who all happen to be educators. I'm in awe when I see people who have been teaching for 20 years wanting to learn new delivery styles, how to teach to various age groups, how to adapt lesson plans to different learner styles and other methodology-type training. Great teachers know when they need to be the student.

Why it's important for educators to keep learning:
- **Motivation.** Watch a TED talk when you get home from work, read an inspirational book or find a local/national conference. You need to be doing something to build your

motivation. It's tough to motivate a classroom full of people day after day. Isn't it possible that you need the same?

- **Networking.** Sometimes you may feel like you're on an island, but you're not. I chair an educator's alliance where we plan several events throughout the year. It's amazing how I see the same individuals in attendance year after year. I often think they should be teaching me. But I know why they're there. Yes, it's to learn something new, but for the most part they want the connection with other educators. They want to know that someone across the country is also having a hard time with attendance. They want to know that this career is important and that there are others who care as much as they do.

- **Technology is moving fast.** Your students are on social media and smartphones—how are you connecting to them? Learning how to use technology in the classroom has to be a priority for every educator. Don't use your ignorance as an excuse. You owe it to your students to stay up on current trends.

- **Leadership and business skills.** You don't have to teach accounting to know the importance of balancing a checkbook. You already have a job, so why learn how to build a resume in the 21st century? Brushing up on life skills is important when you're a mentor to students. You're molding the minds of future professionals. Don't short them by only teaching the textbook. Being well-rounded in various areas will help you answer questions effectively.

- **World events.** If you're in fashion, you need to know what trends are coming next season. If you're in politics, you need to know what boycotts took place this past weekend. Educators need to know what's new and happening in the field they teach. Know what the job market trends are, the different career paths your students can take and current news that could impact that trade.

6
Carolism #2
Great coaches know why their players joined the team.

"Coaches who can outline plays on a blackboard are a dime a dozen. The ones who win get inside their players and motivate them." – Vince Lombardi

Twenty different students will have 20 different reasons why they decided to go to school, but you'll discover a bond. Maybe it's that they want a better life, more money, stability or flexibility.

When a student enrolls in higher education, especially in a school to acquire a specific trade, they have to go through leaps and bounds to enroll. No one just walks through the door, hands over $15,000 and says, *"Can I start tomorrow?"* There is a process and, at most schools, the admissions office is working closely with each prospective student and finding out their personal "why."

When you know why each of your players joined the team, you can better lead that team. You'll be able to know where to spend your time, where you'll be wasting it and how you can better help each player achieve their goal.

If you are being challenged with a difficult student—find out their "why." In my experience, when a student has that dream in front of them, their attitude is better. When their motivation drops, you'll know how to pick them back up.

I like to find out everyone's "why" on the first day of class. At this point they have no low test scores discouraging them, no horrible attendance record hanging over their head—they are ready to jump in and achieve their dreams.

I like doing a snowball fight. Have them each write down their name, why they enrolled and what they want to do one day. Have them crumble it up and throw it around the room. Have each person pick up a "snowball" and introduce someone else in the class.

Why you need to know the "why":

- **You'll avoid snide remarks.** Maybe you don't think a certain career is attainable, realistic or even a good idea. If you know a student in your class wants to do that one day, you'll know not to make insensitive, snide remarks about that career path. Mentioning your personal opinion about someone's dream in a negative manner will hurt that student's chance of succeeding. You need to believe in your team!

- **You can teach to that.** Once you know exactly why everyone is there, you can better tailor your lesson plans. If you're a baseball coach, you bring bats and baseballs to practice—not a football. If you're teaching journalism and you know seven of your students want to be a network news anchor, bring in a local news anchor as a guest speaker or talk about networks who have hired graduates from your school.

- **Body language will mean something.** You need to closely watch for any signals that might lead you to think a student is struggling. Once you detect it, you'll be able to pick them back up by referencing their "why." Here's an example:
  "I noticed you've been late three times in the past two weeks. I know things happen, but you need to realize that others don't take so kindly to this. I know you want to be a cosmetologist because of the flexibility, but if you're late for your appointments, you will lose clients. I know several people who lost their booth space and clients because they took their time getting to work. Flexible doesn't mean time revolves around you. You have to do better."

Some students won't open up or let you in, but as an educator it's imperative that you at least know why they came to school. Get to know your players if you want to lead your team to a win!

7
Carolism #3
Make them curious … and they will come.

Kevin Costner built a baseball field and dead baseball players came. Although I can't guarantee the same results of resurrecting the dead, I can testify to having students show up early for class, eager to learn. Why? Because I had built my class to be somewhere students wanted to be. If you make them curious … they will come.

Later in this book you'll find a chapter dedicated to attendance issues and students being late for class. This is a nation-wide, never-ending problem that I think every single educator has dealt with. In that chapter I talk about the importance of content at the beginning and end of each class. I want to delve into that a bit deeper and give you some concrete takeaways.

How to make your students curious:

- **Make it personal.** You could tease tomorrow's class with what chapters you're covering or with topics you'll be discussing, but you have to show the value to them.

    EXAMPLE: *"Next Friday there will be a test and tomorrow morning we'll be covering the content that the essay questions come from."* Whoa, now they have a reason to be there—they don't want to fail. Do your classes always cover content that could be on a test? Of course, but you have to spell it out. Make it personal.

    EXAMPLE: *"Tuesday's guest speaker told me her company is looking for two summer interns. Wouldn't it be great to hand her a resume in person?"* Teasing your content is one thing—making it about your students is another. It's a learned skill that you should be practicing.

- **Win the crowd.** *"I wasn't the best because I killed quickly. I was the best because the crowd loved me. Win the crowd, win your freedom."* This is one of my favorite lines from the movie "Gladiator" and, believe it or not, perfectly describes a teacher (without that whole killing part).

  You want to win a student? Win the class. Your lesson plans need to incorporate something that students will talk about outside of the classroom—and those who weren't there will feel like they missed out. Maybe you swap a test with an in-class game of Jeopardy. Maybe you host a talk show where your guests are your students pretending to be a professional in the career they're looking to go into. Just do something that will get them excited and will get them taking pictures, recording video and sharing it on social media. Those who missed class will quickly be sorry they did.

- **Give them the unexpected.** It's not a bad thing to be known as the teacher who gives pop quizzes. Back when I was in school I never missed a class if I knew that teacher gave pop quizzes.

  Switch up the classroom layout. Have a student teach for an hour. Show them funny YouTube videos that align with your class material. Give them silly prizes for getting an answer to a question right. If you do the same thing every class then you're giving your students a reason to not be there. Keep your students wondering what you'll be doing tomorrow and suddenly they'll find a reason to skip the snooze button and just hop out of bed.

Let me remind you—it's the curiosity that will keep them wanting to come. You can give punishments for latecomers or no-shows, but no one likes going to places where they're forced to be at. Get your students excited about your classroom and start giving them a reason to show up. They will come … it's just up to you to intrigue them.

8
Carolism #4
Adapt to the student. Don't make them adapt to you.

I'm a storyteller in the classroom. I love to use personal stories about my kids, grandkids, where I grew up, holidays, etc., and then relate those stories to whatever we're talking about in class. But I couldn't do that the year I had "Greg."

Greg came to class quiet, reserved and covered in tattoos. The other students called him "Lurch." He was very tall and would just sit in his desk and not say a word. He didn't make an effort to get to know anyone.

But what Greg didn't know was that I knew him. He was the nephew of my mother's next-door neighbor. I had actually seen him several times over the years. I knew he was a former drug addict and that he was busted for selling drugs and spent time in prison. But I also knew if Greg had an inkling that I knew him, he'd probably drop out of cosmetology school. To him, this was a safe place—a place where no one knew his past, couldn't judge him for past mistakes and had a clean slate.

I never treated Greg differently than any other student, but I did have to throw a bunch of my stories out the window. Anything that could connect me to him would be a disaster. On Greg's first day on the student salon floor, he did the hair of a little, old lady who gave him a tip. With tears in his eyes he showed me that tip and said it was the first honest dollar he had ever made.

Great teachers can sense when their students need something different, even if that means you have to bend your lesson plans or teaching style.

It's not about you—it's about the student. As educators we have to learn how to be flexible and adapt to what our class needs.

How to adapt to your student:

- **Know their triggers.** I have a box full of goodies—cheap, junk machine type items. Each student picks out one item and tells the class why they picked it. I once had a student who chose a white mini beanie baby. She said it was either that or the other item, which was red, and she HATED red. She went into an entire story about how red makes her angry. What did I learn from that? That entire year I never graded a paper with a red pen or used red markers on my whiteboards or flipcharts.

- **Let people have a choice.** I might have a hard time getting through to a student who simply won't pay attention and is never prepared for tests. I know they'd do better on the front row away from distractions, so I let them choose any seat on the first row. If they're constantly forgetting the test day, let them choose which day for the class to take the test next week. Now they feel like everything is on their terms and that they're in control. Adapt to your class by letting them make decisions.

- **Change it up.** Maybe you've always taught a certain chapter one way, but this class has a shorter attention span than normal so you have to switch your delivery method. Never do anything just because it has worked in the past. No two classes are the same.

Having a sense of awareness is the best way to adapt to your student, because now you know what their needs are. Don't ignore problems—face them head on. Be flexible and get creative.

9
Carolism #5
Embrace change. Always.

I couldn't possibly write a Carolism without addressing the importance of change. I talk about this a lot when I educate teachers. By nature, we hate change. We are creatures of habit and set in our ways. But change is a good thing and we have to learn to start embracing it. Change is what gave us freedom. Change is how elections are won. Change is why your kids will have more than you did. Change is the new black!

- **Cell phones.** It's time we start saying "yes" to cell phones in the classroom. I have an entire chapter about incorporating cell phones into your class, so I'm not going to go deeper into it, but I will say it's the number one hesitation I see teachers having today. Change it now. You can't be stubborn forever. One of these days you'll have to switch on that light switch to light a room instead of using a candle.

- **Tablets/laptops.** Note taking can be done electronically. Most students can type faster than they can write. Allowing laptops and tablets is something many teachers are doing, but many aren't. I know you're thinking your students will use this time to surf the Internet or do personal-related stuff online—but as a teacher it's up to you to set those boundaries. Walk your classroom and make sure they're on task.

- **Power Point.** We have the luxury of skipping the blackboard and overhead. We get to use a Power Point presentation! That means no more long, boring paragraphs. Power Point presentations can use color, pictures and video—so why in the world are we filling our slides with boring textbook quotes? Our students have a textbook. Use your Power Point to coincide with your content, not repeat it. You might be used to using it the same way you did your overhead charts. Stop it. Photos and video should be the bulk of your slide content.

- **Lectures.** Get rid of your lecture classes. They're not working. They actually never did, we just didn't know any better. Classes should be animated, fun and full of student participation. If you're the only voice that's heard in that classroom, then no wonder kids are showing up late. You want to bring excitement? You want test scores to go up? Quit the lecture-style teaching.

Change is the only way you'll reach the present and future generations. Let your students teach you something, like maybe a new app you didn't know about. Make them feel valuable. You don't have to have it all figured out. I learn from my students every day and that doesn't make me a poor teacher. It makes me approachable and it gives students value.

I am excited to see so many "old school" teachers embrace technology and embrace change. That is exactly what every great educator needs to be doing. Welcome change and make it happen. After all, change is the new black!

Main Course: The Meat—Carolisms pt. 1
TAKEAWAYS

Ouch! Areas that stepped on my toes

_____

_____

_____

_____

Something new I learned that I didn't know before

_____

_____

_____

_____

Things I will change immediately (because change is the new black!)

_____

_____

_____

_____

10
Carolism #6
Teach your students, but work your room.

"A teacher has two jobs. Fill young minds with knowledge—yes—but more important, give those minds a compass so that that knowledge doesn't go to waste."
– Mr. Holland's Opus

I've been guilty of staying up all night preparing material for tomorrow's lesson. I get to school early to print off my handouts, I've practiced how I'm going to pronounce certain terms and what stories I'll use to make it relatable. I've found myself putting so much emphasis in creating content for knowledge that I didn't consider the compass.

This is something all educators will develop over time. We'll learn the hard way when we give a test, confident that our students know the answers, and then during the grading process we're faced with the reality that we failed them.

This is why I talk so much about delivery methods. Delivery is key to moving that compass and too many teachers are teaching without working their room.

How to work your room:
- **Know your space.** Before the school year, you need to know the layout of the classroom, the view from sitting in each desk, what your voice sounds like in the room, what the Power Point looks like in the morning versus the afternoon depending on when the sun shines through the window, where you can walk

and where you can't. If you're going to work the room, you need to know it.

- **Be animated.** If you're going to stand at the front, deliver content so that everyone feels your energy. Working your room is so much more than where you place your desks. Work it with voice inflection, hand movements, facial gestures and movement. Don't become a talking head by standing behind a podium.

- **Class participation.** Be a sporadic teacher who will pop-quiz your students out loud in the middle of a lesson. While I'm teaching any subject, I might say, *"Katie, give me an example where that might happen to you in the workplace."* You have got to keep the attention of your students by involving them all day long.

- **Activities.** Teach a lesson, take a test, move on to the next chapter. This is how I learned in school…and I hated it. Incorporate activities each day, even if it's a small one like getting them to hop on their phones and find five images on Google relating to a topic you're studying. Activities to correspond with your lesson plans are a must for every great teacher.

Find a balance between teaching and delivery and you'll quickly discover how to move that compass. Working your room is the line separating good teachers from great ones.

Your goal is to teach your students, but showing up every day isn't enough anymore. That little extra effort you put into your lessons will make a giant difference in the lives of your students.

11
Carolism #7
Don't teach to the test. Teach for understanding.

Al Capone died of syphilis. Students might not remember a textbook answer to everything, especially the more complex chapters, but they'll remember a story. It's the very reason why kids learn the alphabet by singing a song. Whenever I teach the dreaded "bacteria" chapter, my students will be able to tell you about the famous mob boss who died of syphilis.

Time and time again I see this problem in schools all across America. Educators have got to quit teaching to the test! This does our students no good. It doesn't help them retain the information long-term and does a poor job preparing them for real-life situations.

This is especially difficult for newer teachers because they may not have enough life experience or they want to prove themselves as an effective teacher by their students testing well. Let's start graduating students who really know the content and will become successful professionals. This is the ultimate goal!

How to teach for understanding:

- **Explain the why.** The bacteria class might not be interesting, but when I explain that you could seriously harm a client or yourself if proper sanitation doesn't take place, they now understand why they need to know this. If our elementary teachers had told us that math would help our problem-solving skills or that knowing the history of this country will explain why men often get paid more than women—then we would've had our "why" answered.

- **Give connectors.** You've got to make the content connect to the student to help them understand it. *"Do you remember a time in your life when…"* or *"Have you ever…"* The content will relate to each student differently. You've just got to help them uncover how it connects to them.

- **Make it come alive.** How do you read "Green Eggs and Ham" to a 5-year-old? You probably use different voices and inflection to make the story come alive. I'm not sure what grade our students were in when story telling became boring, but we've got to be delivering content in that animated, fun way we used to. Make the textbook chapters come alive! It's easier for us to process when it's delivered in a creative way.

Teaching for understanding will make those test grades go up. But more importantly, you'll be giving your students the knowledge that will sustain them well after graduation and into their careers.

12
Carolism #8
Allow your students to make mistakes.

Anyone who has never made a mistake has never tried anything new.
– Albert Einstein

Mistakes will happen; students will cry; they'll want to quit; you'll want to quit. Because mistakes are inevitable, I decided a long time ago that I would allow them and celebrate them. In fact, each student gets to create a "mistake dance" (but mine's the best, of course). When we make a mistake, we do our little dance and move on.

I had a student several years ago who taught me one of the biggest lessons I ever learned. "Katy" was an all-star student. She tried hard, did well and we got along great. Katy never complained about anything, but every Friday her mom would march into my classroom and chew me out for treating Katy unfairly.

It honestly made no sense to me, but I took it. I never asked Katy why her mom was continuing to do it—I just dealt with it. Years later I received a bouquet of flowers the week of Mother's Day with a card that read: *To the second most influential woman in my life. Love, Katy.*

When I called to thank her I finally asked her why her mom came in each week to beat me up for treating her unfairly when we both knew that wasn't the case. She explained that enrolling in cosmetology school wasn't easy for her parents and they were unsupportive of the decision to begin with. Each night she'd come home and make up stories about how horrible I was to her, that way if she failed, her parents would blame me—not her. She couldn't face disappointing them again if she didn't succeed.

Your students have a bigger, overwhelming fear when they make mistakes. They're disappointing themselves, their family and their friends. The fact is, we never know what a student is going through personally, so while everyone is depending on them to succeed, you need to let them make mistakes.

My rules for mistakes:

- **Learn from it.** If you're going to make a mistake, learn what you did wrong and move on. Mistakes aren't intended to be repeated.

- **Own it.** This is not a time to shift the blame or lie about it. Educators and students shouldn't be justifying their mistakes—they should own it. *"I'm sorry, that was my fault. It won't happen again."*

- **Take risks.** You'll notice students taking bigger risks when they know there's no judgment and that you've created a safe environment for them. If you emphasize mistakes are OK, then encourage them to take risks. The fact is they'll be in a job one day where maybe their boss isn't so lenient. I let students know that if they're going to screw up, better now than later.

- **Don't give up.** Once you've created a culture where mistakes are expected, remind your students that it's never a reason to give up. Some will make mistakes weekly, while others will make them daily … and that's OK! Mistakes aren't a reason to quit.

I do want to point out that while mistakes are OK, offending someone or causing emotional pain isn't. Lashing out, being violent or just plain being a bully isn't just a mistake—it's a poor choice. Let your students know that if this occurs, there will be consequences.

Mistakes can be a great thing. We develop into who we are by screwing up. Continue to make mistakes and move on.

13
Carolism #9
Celebrate the success of your students.

We all have bad days. There will be those days when it seems nothing can go right. Sometimes we can be so critical of ourselves that we fail to see the good we accomplish.

At the end of the day in my classroom, each student picks one thing they did well and we celebrate it. If you only see the bad, you'll have a hard time appreciating those tiny instances when everything came together. Remember to celebrate your success.

I once had a student who couldn't hold his comb. I know it sounds crazy for cosmetology school, but this student never once combed hair—not even his own. Something so simple and trivial that everyone else had already mastered, another simply couldn't do.

When he learned how to part hair with a comb, the entire class celebrated. This is the thing about celebrating success—it doesn't have to be a giant feat or even something the majority would think is a big deal.

Someone will get excited over a 71 on a test, while others won't be satisfied without a 90. A win is a win—no matter how great or small. Celebrate them all. What gets recognized gets repeated. It's why experts say to reinforce good behavior as opposed to harping on the bad.

When we get through a tough subject, we have a BYOB (bring your own banana) split party. I have long ago learned that you never know what someone is going through. You never know someone's past, what led them to your classroom or what they're dreading to go home to. If you fail to celebrate their successes, they won't celebrate them either.

We are charged with being the coach of our students, their teammate and their cheerleader. Give them the encouragement they need by celebrating their success.

14
Carolism #10
Cheer them on! Be a dream maker, not a dream stealer.

With every roll of the eyes, every smile turned sad, every snarky comment—you become a dream stealer. Picture a classroom full of naïve students (this isn't too hard to do). You missed your morning coffee because you were running late, the pants you wanted to wear were sitting wet in the washer, you locked your tiny apartment door and realized you forgot to feed your dog and you get in your car only to realize your husband left the tank empty. You pull into the school parking lot just in time to run inside and start your class.

Now you're standing in front of your students, wishing you were any place but there, staring at people who you would trade places with in a second. Right then you overhear a young lady tell her friend, *"If I'm not a millionaire by the time I'm 30, I'll kill myself."*

Every part of you wants to walk over to that ignorant, never-worked-for-anything, wide-eyed young girl and tell her, *"Then you better go ahead and kill yourself because chances of that happening are slim."*

Don't. Don't be the dream stealer. Don't bring someone into a sinkhole just because you don't think they can achieve it or because you aren't even close. You tell her, *"That sounds like a terrific plan. I hope you've been studying hard!"*

Being the dream maker isn't easy. We've got to swallow our pride and come to grips with the fact that we'll be graduating kids who will make more money than us in a few years. We'll be graduating kids whose parents are paying cash for their school (aren't they lucky?). We'll be graduating kids who will change the world ... and we had a hand in that! This isn't something to wallow in. It's something to get excited about!

How to turn "dream stealer" scenarios around:

- **A student gets excited over a less than average accomplishment.** The fact is their terrible grade could be a huge feat for them. Don't ruin their moment. Let them celebrate it and encourage them to continue improving.

- **A student wants a cruise ship spa job.** Yeah ... don't we all? We all have those students who want the career that only has a small hole of open spots. Tell those students, *"There are limited opportunities in that field, so start emailing cruise lines now! Maybe by the time you graduate, or soon after, something will open up!"* You have got to stay positive and give them advice to achieve their dreams.

- **They want to own a business.** This new generation of students wants to jump straight to the top. They come out of school wanting to own a business immediately. We all know this isn't a great plan for a new graduate. The risk, the debt, the list goes on, but you can't be a dream stealer. Try an approach like this: *"That is a great long-term goal! I also think it's completely doable. But let's also consider some short-term goals that will help you be a successful owner. The world's best entrepreneurs gained real-life experience first."*

I see students dropping out of school every year because of their teachers. When educators are so focused on being the disciplinarian (like getting on to a student for being five minutes late) and not focused on making dreams come true, it's discouraging. You become the educator no one wants to be around. You make the industry look boring and terrifying.

Let's start making our students feel like we're their biggest cheerleaders and maybe, just maybe, they'll reach those dreams a bit quicker.

Main Course: The Meat—Carolisms pt. 2
TAKEAWAYS

Ouch! Areas that stepped on my toes

_____

_____

_____

_____

Something new I learned that I didn't know before

_____

_____

_____

Things I will change immediately (because change is the new black!)

_____

_____

_____

_____

DESSERT
Sweet Tips to Satisfy You

15
What If Your Student is Older Than You?

I can still remember "Janet's" first day. She simply didn't fit in. She was a recently retired, well-educated woman who decided at the age of 63 to enroll in cosmetology school. The other students around her automatically seized her up as a "cranky old lady."

What do you when your student is older than you? For an educator, this is an increasing trend that you'll have to face year after year. Enrollment of students 25 years or older increased 42 percent between 2000 and 2010 according to the National Center for Education Statistics. Educators often get scared when they walk in the door and see a student who is older than their own mother or father.

Here are some things you have to remember:

- **They know they're older.** They knew it before they enrolled; they knew it before they drove to school; they knew it before you walked in the door.

- **Don't assume they're a know-it-all.** They're sitting in your classroom because they have already come to grips with the fact that they need to learn something.

- **They're scared.** They haven't been in school in a while, so they're already terrified you're going to bring out something new and tech-savvy that they can't keep up with.

- **Age has nothing to do with the ability to learn.** No matter how old someone is—you can teach them something!

- **They're more "ready" than the majority of your other students.** You don't get up and decide at 50+ you want to give college a try. You do that at 18. Older students have prepared themselves, have clear, defined goals and are ready to jump in and be successful.

What you can do:

- **Learn their story.** Many of Janet's friends and family were in a nursing home and all she wanted to do was become licensed in cosmetology so she could pamper the residents. Once you know their reason for being there, you can constantly use this as a reminder when they need encouragement or motivation.

- **Make them feel comfortable.** Avoid offensive terms like "seasoned" or "older" when referring to them in your classroom. Whatever you do, put yourself in their shoes and don't ever let them feel like they don't belong.

- **Make them your helper.** Older students are caregivers by nature. From making copies to putting notes on the board, find little ways to involve them in your class where they feel important and like they have purpose.

- **Earn their respect.** Be as subtle as possible. When you're trying to involve them, don't say, *"Would you like to be my helper today?"* Try, *"If you have a minute can you help me?"* This, in time, will help you earn their respect.

When Janet graduated, she hadn't just changed my perception of older students—she changed everyone's. She received a standing ovation on graduation day from her fellow classmates.

Having a student who is older than you can be quite intimidating, but remember your main purpose—to prepare students for their future. Age really is just a number.

16
The Importance of Thank You

What do you do when a quiet student with low self-confidence finally raises their hand and answers a question you've asked the class … and they get it wrong? I answer them the exact same way I would if a student became extremely angry and started voicing their frustrations. I use two small words that make a big impact—thank you.

"Thank you" is my best fire extinguisher in the classroom. It's the one phrase that can calm someone down, build someone back up and make someone feel important.

The importance of thank you is something that separates good teachers from great. Good teachers say thank you when they are validated—great teachers understand the importance of using it to validate someone else. It's a minimal gesture that makes a huge difference.

When you say *thank you*, you are saying:

- I heard you
- I appreciate you
- You are important enough for me to listen to you

When emotions run high, intelligence is low. When someone reacts with high emotion (like in a rage), saying "thank you" knocks them right off their game and causes them to not know how to respond.

That's why when I have a student who wants to tell me how the universe hates them, I respond, *"Thank you for trusting me enough to tell me how you feel."* It immediately brings their emotional rage down a level. You can either play into it or say thank you.

When a student, any student really (not just the type in the example above) answers a question wrong, I say, *"Thank you! You're not quite there; does anyone else want to add to that?"* Now instead of them feeling bad about their wrong answer, you've just validated them to make them feel appreciated for even trying.

Saying thank you creates a safe environment, it shows your students that you respect them and it adds to the value of your classroom culture. Do you have a fire you're battling in class? Say thank you and watch it burn out.

17
Teaching the Auditory Learner

Auditory learners can be a challenge for several educators. However, the problem isn't with those types of students—it's with the teacher. It's up to us to adapt our lesson plans for all types of learners and look at it from their perspective.

An auditory learner is one who learns through listening. They process through their ears. In order for them to understand information, they have to physically hear what is being said otherwise they won't grasp it. (As opposed to visual learners who can see an example of something and learn it that way.)

Indicators you have an auditory learner in your class:

- You think a student isn't paying attention, yet they always know the answer when you call on them.
- Their head may down or they may be doodling.
- They test well (good at oral exams or written responses).
- They problem-solve by talking it through.
- They move their lips or talk to themselves as they're doing something.
- Their words indicate listening over watching. They use phrases like, *"I hear you,"* or *"I'm can't wait to hear what you'll be speaking about."*
- They can listen to music and still focus.

With auditory learners you need to watch:

- **Your words.** Don't say, *"Look at me,"* or suggest everyone put their pens down and focus on you while you're speaking. It takes auditory learners extra time to focus on you, when in reality they can hear you just fine without looking.

- **Your presentation-style.** Don't have visually-centered classes all the time. Although some require demonstrations or a Power Point, be sure you're still using words to talk through your demos or slides.

- **Assumptions.** Don't assume you're being ignored or that your students are being disrespectful by making little to no eye contact.

How to teach to auditory learners:

- **Use tone and pitch.** Auditory learners respond to changes in tone and they find meaning in words by picking up on these signals. Be sure your tone and pitch reflect what you're trying to say.

- **Get them to actively participate.** If auditory learners want to remember an address, they can't just look at it on Google Maps. They have to say the address out loud. Get them to answer orally in a class setting to ensure they understood your message.

- **Put on some music.** Although this can be distracting for other students, find times to introduce background noise for auditory learners. Let them thrive in your classroom.

Unsure what learning styles you have in your classroom? Have your students take a free quiz online to find out. (There are several out there.) Remember: how you learn is how you study. Don't teach to your learning style—adapt to your students.

18
Cell Phones: The #1 Battle You'll Never Win

When Thomas Edison invented the light bulb, some refused to embrace his life-altering invention and continued to light their rooms with candlelight. How well equipped would we be today if our teachers were so anti-technology that they refused to teach us how to type on a typewriter or computer?

If you're not integrating cell phones in the classroom you are crippling your students.

Cell phones are how we communicate with the world today. When you ask a student to lock up their phone, you're telling them that their sick daughter at home isn't important, or that their dad's surgery outcome doesn't matter, or that you really don't care about anything in their life outside of your classroom.

How do we know our students are using their phones? Their heads are down, their hands are under the table and they all touch their pockets at the sound of a vibration.

If you require cell phones to be locked up, you're giving your students so much anxiety that they simply won't be able to concentrate. This is a battle you aren't going to win, so quit fighting it!

My rules for cell phones in the classroom:

- **They must be on silent, not vibrate.** We all know our ringtones. If you hear a phone ring and it's not your ringtone, you simply don't care and ignore it. If a phone vibrates, everyone looks for their phone, thinking it could be theirs. My rule is to turn the phone to silent.

- **Put them on the desk upside down.** Students feel at ease just simply having their phone in sight. They can see it and they can feel it—but the screen must be facing down on the desk.
- **Integrate them into your class.** Below I'll share some tips for using them in your class, but make sure your students know that they will get to use them at times. They'll look forward to this.
- **Have them agree to your terms.** My students know these rules. They also know if they break them, they'll forfeit the privilege of using them in the class for that day. I make every student raise his or her hand to agree to my terms. Trust me, if the alternative is to lock them up, they'll agree.
- **Never take away a phone.** This is their personal property. A good teacher can be in control of the class without such harsh punishment. A student would rather you take the keys to their car than to take away their phone. Don't lose their respect by doing this.

Ways to integrate cells phones in the classroom:

- **Instagram.** Have them snap a picture of something they're working on and Instagram the picture using a specific hashtag.
- **Surveys.** Use an online system (like Survey Monkey) to create a survey and share the link with your students to take the survey. This is a great way to get immediate feedback or a way to get statistics to share in a lesson.
- **Facebook.** Find some educational fan pages that are relevant to their learning and have them "like" those pages. You can even discuss some of the content on those pages. You can also set up a private Facebook group for them to join where

students can converse with each other and where you can share homework assignments and relevant information.

- **Search engines.** This is always a great game for students. Ask questions and have them search for the answers online.

When you do these activities, will they quickly view their text messages, check their email and social media notifications? Of course—but who cares? They'll do it so quickly that it usually isn't even a distraction. If they're still participating and following your rules, let it go. This is a battle I simply wouldn't choose.

Be sure you stay within these parameters and hold your students accountable. Our world today is driven by the use of technology. Integrating technology into the classroom will only help them in the long run.

CAROL WOODARD

19
Dealing With a Know-It-All

We've all had them in our class. They've annoyed us, frustrated us and brought out the worst in us. The "know-it-all student" exists in every school and usually ends up in my class every year.

"Holly" always wanted to correct me. She would challenge me, try to one-up me and found pleasure in finding my mistakes and letting the entire class know. I was teaching a cosmetology class and prepping the students for the state board exam when I mentioned that the heel on a shoe couldn't exceed a particular height. Holly shouted out that I was wrong and that her new shoes would be just fine to wear.

I quickly mouthed back, *"You go right ahead and let me know how that works out for you when you have to re-test."* The whole class laughed, but I knew I went over the line the second those words hit my tongue. That's when I discovered that the only thing worse than a know-it-all is a disgruntled know-it-all.

What I've learned about know-it-all students:

- **They actually know less.** This is a control game for the majority of them. Maybe they've had a lifetime of having to prove themselves, but the majority of them simply don't know as much you might think.

- **They want to be heard.** Their main mission is to take over your class and have eyes on them.

- **They can't take humiliation.** These students don't want you to be sarcastic or joke around, especially if they are the center of the joke. They are insecure, vulnerable and can't handle it.

How to deal with know-it-all students:

- **Shut them down.** Don't allow them to ever be in control of your class. Many teachers are afraid they'll be asked a question they don't know the answer to or that the student actually is smarter. This is seldom the case. Nip it from day one and show them that you're the educator.

- **Never embarrass or humiliate them.** You need them to be on your team if you want to make it through the year. Don't make things worse by making them feel terrible. They'll hold it against you and make your life even worse. Give them a chance to show that they're willing to play on your team.

- **Build them up, publicly.** If you drop their name in front of everyone, they won't need to hear their voice. Mention them in a positive way in class. If they're yelling out answers or saying, *"I know, I know,"* say, *"I know that you know and I'm always impressed that you're prepared, but let's give someone else a chance to answer so that I know they prepared as well."*

- **Direct the attention away in a non-threatening way.** Your body language should reflect that you are in charge. You can move your shoulders and feet away from them, addressing other students in the classroom without it appearing like a direct snub.

With Holly, I should've had more grace. I should've told her, *"I love your shoes and I'm hoping they will meet the standards. Let's read those chapters again and then get a ruler to measure the heel just to make sure. I'd hate for you to pass every portion of the test but miss the mark over your shoes."*

I have found all-star students in know-it-alls. They're punctual, they study and they want to prove that they are intelligent. If you can get them on your side, you won't dread these students year after year.

20
Winning the Introvert

If you're a teacher, then you generally don't mind talking to a large group of people. Not all educators are extroverts, but for the most part, we don't tense up when we're called on to talk.

I think that's why introverts find school-type settings so difficult. They hope to God you don't call on them and they seem to want to hide. But the reality is, introverts are observers. They're paying attention probably better than most of the other students and they often perform well on tests.

I had a student named "Doug" and I couldn't for the life of me figure out why he wanted to be a cosmetologist. He hardly participated and making eye contact was like torture for him. How was this guy going to cut hair and talk to people for a living?

I went to the admissions office to get "the scoop" and discovered he was a single father to two daughters and wanted a stable career to take care of them. I made it my mission to learn more about Doug so that he would be successful in my classroom.

How to win the introvert:

- **Take away the fear.** Most of the time there is something preventing them from completely opening up. Whether it's at home, self-image, whatever—you need to create a safe space without judgment. They don't trust you yet. You have to earn it.
- **Don't call them out.** Sometimes even saying their name will embarrass them. If they're going to participate, it needs to be

on their terms—not yours. Don't bring up bad memories if you know their history. Position yourself toward them so they feel included.

- **Find a connection.** When I discovered that Doug rode that motorcycle parked out front, I brought it up in class. I said, *"Wow, that is the coolest bike. Did anyone else see it? I wonder whose it is."* Then he, on his own terms, piped up and said it was his. He immediately got excited and told the whole class about it. It was at that moment that Doug finally had a connection to his peers and me.

- **Don't change them.** It's not about making an introvert and extravert. It's about building their trust and helping them succeed no matter who they are, what kind of learner they are or what their history is. That's your job as a teacher—to bring out the best in everyone.

MAKE THE RECIPE YOUR OWN!
Dessert: Sweet Tips to Satisfy You
TAKEAWAYS

Ouch! Areas that stepped on my toes

_____

_____

_____

Something new I learned that I didn't know before

_____

_____

_____

Things I will change immediately (because change is the new black!)

_____

_____

_____

_____

COFFEE
Finishers to Take You to the Next Level

21
Are You the Reason Your Students Are Late?

If you had a job interview, would you be late? If you had an important doctor's appointment, would you leave early to make sure you're on time? Over and over again I hear teachers unite over one universal complaint: students show up late!

Whether it's traffic or a family problem, we all hear the same excuses year after year. Yes, some of them are legitimate, but for the most part, it's the same students who continually disrespect the importance of punctuality.

In my years of teaching I've learned one major thing in regards to students showing up late for class, and it's not easy to hear. It's not the student's fault. It's the teacher's.

Ask yourself these questions:

- **Are you starting class on time?** If you're not showing that time is important to you, then it won't be to your students. If class starts at 8 a.m., be sure you as the teacher are there on time and that you're starting class at 8 a.m. sharp.

- **What do you cover in the first 5 – 10 minutes?** If you're doing nothing but roll call and waiting for late ones to arrive—you're not giving your students a reason to be on time. Try giving substance right off the bat. Maybe give hints for an upcoming test, ways they can earn extra credit or details about an upcoming project. Or, if you're doing group work that day, put them into groups as soon as class starts. Once your students catch on to the importance of the first five minutes of class, they will make it a point to be there.

- **Are you praising the good or are you punishing the bad?** Instead of showing how annoyed you are when someone walks in late, show public appreciation for the ones who are there on time. The best way to get consistently good behavior is to reward those who meet your expectations—not punish the ones who don't.

- **Are you closing with a teaser?** Your students may not all be there at the beginning of class, but they are at the end. Be sure to tease tomorrow's "opener" to give your students another reason to not hit that snooze button the next morning.

The next time you find yourself frustrated with students who can't tell time as well as you can, be sure to analyze yourself to ensure that you aren't the problem. We aren't perfect and if there are ways we can help our students succeed (or even be on time), we should be taking those opportunities.

22
How Do You Serve Your Mashed Potatoes?

Have you ever watched a made-for-TV movie and thought it was laughable, yet a Hollywood version of the same story line moved you to tears? It's the same reason one teacher can have students that test well, yet another can't.

If it's Thanksgiving and I buy KFC mashed potatoes and put the container right out of the bag onto the table, it's just fast food. Now, if I take those same potatoes and put them in a crystal serving bowl, it becomes a side-dish to a perfect Thanksgiving dinner.

It's not the content—it's the delivery. How are you serving your mashed potatoes?

Indicators that you're serving fast food:
- Attendance has dropped
- Students find excuses to leave early
- Students take lots of bathroom breaks
- Consistently low test scores
- Poor class participation
- Passion is lacking in your students
- Your Power Point slides have more words than pictures
- You've been teaching content the same way year after year

Tips to successful delivery (serve it up!):

- **Become student-focused.** It's time to quit using boring, complicated chapters in the textbook as an excuse for a dull lesson plan. A teacher needs to become student-focused, not self-focused. How would you want to learn a less than exciting topic? Maybe with a live presentation? Perhaps with a group project? Make it interesting and always be thinking of ways your students might learn a subject better.

- **Know your learner styles.** You have auditory, visual and kinesthetic learners in your classroom. Find out who learns what way and teach to that. There are ways to incorporate all of these learning styles into your lesson plans, so be creative. Don't teach to one specific group every time. You have to adapt to the learning preference of your students.

- **Be animated.** All three learning styles respond to an animated teacher. Use voice inflection, humor and real-life examples. There is nothing worse than a boring, monotone talking head.

- **Change is the new black.** This is my motto for a reason. We, as teachers, have got to rid our old-school methods and embrace change! Our students crave it and will never learn if we don't get innovative. Make things exciting by changing up your classes and your students will quickly learn that your unpredictability is reason enough to show up.

Let's focus less on the content (because we already know that stuff!) and spend more time honing our delivery methods. We're charged with the task of educating new students each year. Let's serve it up!

23
Grading 101

Tests aren't generally something people look forward to. As a teacher, I love them! When you think about it, tests are the best way to gauge how well you've taught something (or how well you didn't).

I talk about this a lot when I speak, but one of the biggest mistakes teachers make is teaching to the test. The goal isn't for our students to get every answer correct. The goal is for them to be successful one day in their careers. Telling your students word for word test questions ahead of time doesn't help them when they've graduated and are in the field.

I see teachers all the time who grade to be popular. They give everyone 100's and they're everyone's best friend. You're creating lazy students when you do this. You're not setting them up to aim high and achieve more. Your grades need to have value otherwise you're crippling them. You need to have a standard and stick to it.

You'll have students who ace exams and others who fail. You'll find some students don't have to study at all and others who will end up cramming all night. What's important is that your grading rules are consistent.

My rules for grading and testing:

1. Answers should be direct. Don't leave things up to interpretation. You need to have clear reasons as to why they scored high or low.

2. Trick questions are mean. I hated when my teachers used these and your students will hate you too.

3. Expect more out of students who have been in school longer.
4. Don't grade papers in red. It's harsh and can hurt someone's self-image. I like grading in green or blue.
5. Open-book or take-home tests create lazy students. They're searching for the answers—they're not learning to understand.
6. If a lot of your students miss a specific question, the responsibility falls on you. Take a look at the way you taught that subject and find a more effective way to communicate it.
7. Allow some form of make-up tests, even if they're absent or late. Have a policy that there will be consequences like a certain amount of points off.
8. Extra credit is not a good way to make-up for bad test scores. The fact is if they didn't know the information, they still need to. Allowing them to do something else that they already know how to do doesn't help them.
9. Don't let students grade each other's papers. That is a sign of a lazy teacher. In addition, that grade is private between you and the student.
10. Always give test reviews before an exam.
11. Always review the answers as a class after you've graded the papers. When doing this, allow the students to describe in-depth why they answered a certain way. It may help a student who got it wrong.
12. Have a private conversation with students who continually get bad grades. Use statements like, *"Here's what I noticed when grading your paper,"* and find out what you can do to help them succeed. You need to be their cheerleader.

You should see an array of grades—some should be high and some should be low. Not everyone learns the same or tests the same, so expect grades to be all over the place. What's important is that you see individuals improving.

24
Setting Up Your Classroom to Make You – Not Break You

Sometimes we put so much focus on our teaching methods and lesson plans that we completely forget about our stage—the classroom itself. Your classroom is your biggest serving dish. It is where you are delivering your content; it is where your students interact with each other; it is where the learning takes place; it is where tests will be given. A poor environment can have adverse effects on the development of your students. Set it up to make you—not break you!

For starters, I want to know my classroom like I know my students. Before school even starts, walk your classroom, test out your voice in the space, sit in every seat and determine what you can see, what can't see and take inventory of what your room is lacking that you might need. There are some students who can learn anywhere and in any place. However, this is not the case for most. Where your students sit on the first day of class will most likely be their seat for the whole year. The classroom is their "safe place." Be sure you are giving them an environment and setting that will benefit their learning.

How to set up your classroom:

- **Be sure it's clean.** The reason people love staying in hotels is that they're clutter-free. You'd clean up your house if you were having company. Why wouldn't you do the same for your students? Be sure your classroom is clean, sharp and free from clutter. This would include irrelevant stuff on the walls. Everyone loves an inspirational quote, but if it has little to do with what you're teaching, it can become a distraction to your students.

- **Don't have a seating chart.** Unless you're teaching elementary education, a seating chart for adult students will make them feel like kids. Students will be happier if they're sitting somewhere they chose. Adult learners go to school by choice, so for the most part, they'll automatically sit somewhere that is most beneficial to them.

- **Set up desks in a beneficial way.** I love a U-shaped seating arrangement. It gives everyone a front row seat and I can have personal interaction with every student. It's important to never put desks in a circle if a demonstration is taking place in the center. Someone will be stuck staring at a back. Think about every seat before you set up a classroom. Be sure you can walk by each desk. If your classroom needs to have desks in rows, spread them apart well enough that you can have personal one-on-one interaction if you need.

- **Change it up.** You don't have to keep the room the same all year long. If you're showing a video, be sure the seats are set up in a way where everyone has a great view. If you're doing a live demonstration, make certain all students can see what's going on. Change is dependent upon your lesson plan and the learner styles in your room. Change your room as you see fit.

- **Where is your desk?** If your desk separates the students from the whiteboard up front, the information on the board belongs to you—the teacher. If your desk is at the back of the room or off to the side, suddenly that information on the board belongs to your students. It's not intentional, but where you place furniture, like your desk, can send messages that can hinder the learning of your students.

It might be an after-thought for educators, but the classroom is one of the most important elements to teaching. Be sure you're setting up a room for success.

25
Are You Personally Grounded?

- Are you "friends" with your students on your personal Facebook page?
- Do you tell your students about your romantic relationships?
- Do your students know when you've had a bad day? (Maybe you got pulled over on the way to work, maybe your husband never put your wet clothes in the dryer—do your students know about it?)
- Do you have personal conversations with other staff members in a student environment?
- Have you ever forgotten your lunch and a student loaned you a couple bucks so you wouldn't starve?

If you answered yes to any of these questions, it's an indicator that you're not personally grounded. The moment you're not personally grounded, you've lost your ability to teach effectively. I have seen it time and time again—teachers wanting to be friends with students, students feeling way too comfortable with their teacher, and I'd run out of fingers and toes counting all the educators that I personally know who have lost their job over it.

I am all for embracing change, getting with the times and updating our teaching style to meet 21st century methods, but being personally grounded is a fundamental that cannot be compromised. Once your students become engrossed in your personal life, school becomes a quick number two.

The definition of someone who is personally grounded is someone who has come to terms with whatever has gone on in their own life and can separate it from work.

I think social media is a great way to connect with our students. I strongly urge my educators to have their own "work" profile separate from their personal one. A work profile should not include vacation pictures, family updates or any personal information. Don't give your students a reason to strike up a conversation with you about something personal they saw on your Facebook page. Separate the two.

We all have bad days; I get it. But storming into the class airing your own dirty laundry will only make the students not respect you. Try to find another place to vent that doesn't resemble a classroom.

Although it's OK to have trusted relationships amongst the staff, keep it away from your class settings. A teacher might come up to you and say, *"How are things going with counseling?"* and if a student overhears it, by the end of class rumors are spreading that you have multiple personalities, are suicidal and your husband left you. This is why it's imperative you keep your personal life away from your students.

It may seem harmless that someone would loan you five bucks, but when that student shows up to school not in dress code and you have to send them home, suddenly you get, *"Really? You don't remember that time I lent you lunch money? And this is what I get?"*

If you have a health issue, go to the doctor. If you are having personal problems, I strongly urge you to seek help for it. Balanced teachers are the most effective. But for the sake of your students, become a personally grounded teacher.

26
When Your Student Keeps Failing

Practice doesn't always make perfect. Let's quit telling the lie that it does and start fixing the real problem. If you do something wrong a thousand times, you're not automatically going to get it on the 1001st try. Perfect practice makes perfect. Continued improvement and getting better each time will help you perfect a craft, but it doesn't guarantee success.

We've all had students in our classrooms who are smart and have a lot to offer, but who continually fail. There isn't enough positive reinforcement to turn someone into something they're not. So what do you do when you've got that student sitting in front of you?

When your student is failing:

- **Believe in them.** Don't give up on them yet. This might be their true passion and perhaps in time they'll get the hang of it. Sometimes self-doubt is what's making them fail. Be their cheerleader and believe in them. I have my students chant, *"I can do this! I can do this."* That little exercise does wonders and wipes away self-doubt.

- **Celebrate their improvement.** Once they do something that inches them closer to success, encourage them and keep pushing them to improve. Just because they have to work harder than others doesn't mean they're not cut out for this career. Celebrate every milestone and give them hope.

- **Be open with your failures.** Make your students feel comfortable coming to you to discuss their problems by being open with yours. I may have a cosmetology license, but I'm terrible at doing nails. This is something I tell my students. You don't have to be good at everything—you just have to be good at something.

- **Steer them in another path.** Every industry offers a variety of jobs. It's possible that your struggling student is better suited for a career they're either not aware of or hadn't considered. Point out their positives and help them find something they'd be good at.

Don't ever make a student feel like less of a person if they're failing. The truth is, they already know it and are harder on themselves internally than you could ever be. It's our job as educators to give a student the tools they need to do something they're passionate about.

27
Is Quitting Your Job the Answer?

"Jada" had been working at my school for seven years. The students loved her, she had passion when she taught and she continually worked hard to teach in an easy-to-understand way. Then it seemed like overnight, Jada changed. She started showing up late, complaining about our meetings, claimed we treated her unfairly and that we didn't support her like we used to. After finally taking the time to sit down and hear her out, I discovered her husband had been unfaithful to her.

It's amazing how outside factors can change how you feel about work. What do you do when you're ready to throw in the towel and quit?

There are moments when you'll want to. There are times when walking away seems so much easier than sticking it out. Even if you have a somewhat valid reason to leave your job, don't ever make a rash decision based on emotions.

When I get called in to speak with someone who is thinking about leaving, 80% of the time the root of it is something external—parents, kids, spouse—something outside of the classroom doors. But there are cases when a bad review, a student complaint or an employee fight will cause someone to want to leave. I'm a believer that when the going gets tough, any problem can be worked through.

My rules before you hand in your notice and quit:

- **Identify the problem.** Is an external problem causing this minor work problem to seem major? If something else in your life is the root of your issue, then finding a new job won't fix it.
- **Find someone you can confide in.** Maybe it's another

employee, an HR specialist, a family member or a therapist. Problems need to be talked through. What you need is someone who will listen to you.

- **Make a list of your successes.** It's not fair to punish yourself because one student complained about you. List out your accomplishments, your highs and the reasons you once loved your job. When you've had time to cool down, go back and read this list and see what you'll be missing out on.

- **Write out a new 30-day plan.** So, you want to leave—now what? Where will you go? What will be different this time? What will be your new challenges? The grass isn't always greener on the other side. You might have it better than you think. Writing out a 30-day plan will help you identify how you intend to fix your current situation.

- **Don't quit while you're emotional.** Handing in your notice when you're furious is something you'll regret. Don't burn bridges or do something you're going to have to apologize for later. If you've decided to move on, do it calmly and always leave on good terms.

MAKE THE RECIPE YOUR OWN!

Coffee: Finishers to Take You to the Next Level TAKEAWAYS

Ouch! Areas that stepped on my toes

_____

_____

_____

_____

Something new I learned that I didn't know before

_____

_____

_____

Things I will change immediately (because change is the new black!)

_____

_____

_____

_____

TAKEOUT
Activities to Bring to Class

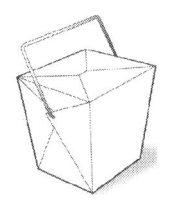

28
Icebreakers

Pick-a-Partner

1. Pair up the students with a classmate.
2. Each student takes a turn telling their partner important things about his or her life (family, hobbies, likes/dislikes, goals, etc.).
3. Go around the room and have each student introduce their partner with a couple interesting facts they learned.

One-Minute Mixer

1. Move the desks out of the way so that students are standing around and can easily move.
2. Have students find a partner and set a timer for one minute.
3. Students should converse and get to know each other until you yell "switch."
4. Repeat until students have met everyone.

Two Truths and a Lie

1. Students should write down two facts about themselves and one lie.
2. Have them share these with the class out loud and let the students vote to determine which one is the lie (before the student reveals which one is a lie).

B-I-N-G-O

1. Distribute a Bingo sheet to each student with 25 general characteristics on it (see below for an example if you teach in post-secondary education).
2. Let the students mingle until they can find students to match those traits. Although a student may match multiple traits, they can only have their name once on someone's paper. (However their name could be written by "Has a Tattoo" on one student's and "Has two Cats" on another student's.)
3. The first one to get five in a row (like in B-I-N-G-O) wins!

HAS 4+ TATTOOS	HAS TWO CATS	DRIVES A HYBRID	CAN'T SWIM	ALLERGIC TO NUTS
DOESN'T WATCH TV	HAS TWO KIDS	WAS BORN OUTSIDE THE U.S.	HAS BEEN ON A CRUISE	HAS SKYDIVED
LIVED IN ANOTHER STATE	PREFERS TEA OVER COFFEE	RAN A MARATHON	PLAYS IN A SPORTS LEAGUE	CAN PLAY AN INSTRUMENT
HAS BEEN TO EUROPE	HAS ZIPLINED	HAS BEEN ON TV	BLOGS REGULARLY	BEEN MARRIED 10+ YEARS
RIDES A MOTORCYCLE	DRIVES 30+ MILES TO SCHOOL	RECENTLY WENT TO A CONCERT	SINGS KARAOKE	HAS A BACHELOR'S DEGREE

The 3 C's (Color, Car and Character)

1. Have each person write down on a piece of paper their name followed by a color that best describes them, their favorite car and a fictional character they identify with.
2. Go around the room and have your students share these with the class.

"I Have Never"

1. Have your students stand or sit in a circle.
2. One student will start in the center and say something they've never done. (For example, "I have never been to Hawaii," or "I have never learned to ride a bike," etc.)
3. Someone sitting in the circle who HAS done that will take their place in the center and share something they've never done (and repeat until multiple people have had a chance in the center).
4. If no one in the circle has done what was said, the person in the center keeps going until someone has.

Pass the Ball to Find Out "Why"

1. Have your students stand in a circle and start with a ball in your hand.
2. Tell the class why you became a teacher and throw the ball to a student.
3. The student will then share why they came to that school (or decided to get into that specific career).
4. Repeat until each student has had the ball and shared their "why."

Variations: You can use this game to have students share hidden talents, embarrassing moments, their favorite TV show, etc. It's also a great activity to use at the end of a unit/subject/chapter. Have each student share something significant they learned.

29
Build Them Up

It's inevitable—your students will have days when they need some motivation. Perhaps something bad happened to a student or a world event shakes the campus. We all have moments when we're down in the dumps and need some lifting up. I find doing monthly activities like this will help keep your students inspired and ready to face challenges.

Pat on the Back

1. Have each student outline their hand on a piece of paper, cut it out and tape it to their back.

2. Let the students go around the room with a pen, writing something nice about each person on the hand on their back.

"I Wish"

1. Have the students sit in a circle and put one student in the center.

2. Go around the circle and let each student share something that they admire about the student in the center. (For example, "I wish I could talk to people the way you do you," or "I wish I could have your determination.")

This activity is good to do weekly with one or two students, as it can be time-consuming. It's also good to put the focus for that day or week on one or two students.

Face Your Fears

Often times it's the fear your students have that will hurt their self-confidence. They fear they won't get a job. They fear they won't provide for their family. They fear they won't succeed. However, there is strength in numbers and it's easier to face fears when you're not alone.

Have each student write down a couple of their fears and share them with the class. You can write them down on a whiteboard as people start to yell out their fears. After you have a list, go through each one and ask people to raise their hand if they also have that fear. It's a great way for students to see that they're not alone.

Then, as an educator, it's up to you to help them face these fears and give them the encouragement they need to succeed.

Guest Speakers

Bringing a guest into your class will always give your students a boost of motivation! Ask successful alum to share their story or invite a professional in the field they're studying to inspire your students. We often forget that listening to the same person each day can become boring. Sometimes a fresh face and voice in the classroom is all your students need to wake up again.

30

Team Building

Your class is a team. More importantly, they'll be joining a team when they graduate, and although we focus a lot of our attention on growing individuals, it's important that we're doing our part in teaching our students how to work as a team. A lot of employee dissatisfaction comes from drama between co-workers, so helping your students work together will go a long way. Team building exercises are also a great way to make classes fun and interesting.

Human Knot

1. Arrange students in a circle, standing and facing each other.
2. When you say, "Go," each student should hold hands with someone standing across from them.
3. The main goal is for the students to untangle themselves by not breaking hands and using communication. This will require teamwork, careful strategy and climbing over each other.
4. If the group cannot untangle themselves within 10 minutes, the team can allow two students to swap their handholding partners or kick someone out of the chain.
5. Every 10 minutes, if the team finds themselves stuck, they can make one the two decisions from #4.
6. Students who are kicked out of the chain may work to help strategize other moves to make.
7. The game is over once the knot is completely untied and the group is a circle once again.

The Bigger Picture

1. Choose a well-known picture or cartoon that is full of detail.
2. Cut into as many equal squares as there are students.
3. Give each student a piece of the "puzzle" and instruct them to create an exact copy of their piece of the puzzle five times bigger than its original size on a larger square piece of paper. (Students are posed with the problem of not knowing why or how their own work affects the bigger picture.)
4. When all the students have completed their enlargements, have them assemble their pieces into a giant copy of the original picture on a table.

Napkin Game

1. Put students in groups of four to six and give each student a cloth napkin.
2. Each student takes a turn for one minute, demonstrating a unique use for the napkin in front of his or hers group—without talking.
3. Students will find interesting and funny ways to use a napkin and they'll learn how to solve problems with minimal communication. Students can even use other group members as "props" for their presentation.

Card Tower

1. Put students in groups of four to six and give each group a deck of cards and scissors.
2. Students must work in their team to create the largest tower use only those items. Students can bend, stack and cut cards.
3. The team with the highest tower after 30 minutes wins.

Umbrella Warehouse

Your class just inherited an umbrella warehouse—in an area that doesn't rain!

1. Break the students up into small groups and have them brainstorm unique, interesting ways you can use umbrellas that will help sell your current inventory.
2. Have each group present their best idea.
3. This activity will help them think outside of the box and be creative.

Blind Drawing

1. Divide your students into pairs. Give one person from the pair a picture of a simple object and the other person a pencil and piece of paper.
2. The student with the picture must give verbal instructions to their partner on how to draw that object—without telling them what the object is.
3. After they're finished, have the partners compare the picture to the drawing.
4. Students should consider how well their description and instructions were and how well they communicated.

Survivor

Twelve people will be stranded on an island for 30 days. Small groups must work together to create a list of 24 items they'll need to survive. After the lists are created, have the students cut it down in half—allowing only 12 items from that list. Each group should present their list and why they chose those items.

Personal Reflections

Why did you become an educator?

_____

_____

_____

Why are you still an educator?

_____

_____

_____

(Consider—how much do these first two answers differ?)

When did you fall in love with your career and know that this is exactly what you should be doing?

_____

_____

_____

Who inspired you to become an educator and what was it specifically that inspired you?

_____

_____

_____

(Have you written them a thank you card to that person?)

PERSONAL REFLECTIONS

When was the first time you were seriously challenged?

_____

_____

(How difficult would that challenge be today?)

Describe a memorable "breakthrough moment." (When you finally got something that had seemed impossible.)

_____

_____

(Remember how good that felt?)

Name a time you didn't support a student in the way you should have.

_____

_____

(We've all been dream stealers at some point. Let's be dream makers!)

Name a time when you supported a student who needed that extra push and they exceeded everyone's expectations. How did that make you feel?

_____

_____

(You are powerful influence!)

In what ways have you changed your teaching techniques to adapt to technological advances?

_____

_____

_____

(Change is the new black!)

What subject do you dread teaching and how can you make it more fun for your students?

_____

_____

_____

(Think about the student and how they want to learn the information.)

What teaching technique or method are you really great at that you could share with another educator?

_____

_____

_____

(Let's help newer, less-experienced educators.)

PERSONAL REFLECTIONS

What is a quick way to mess up your day and get you in a bad mood?

_____

_____

_____

(Can your students tell? Let's leave it at the door.)

Name a few students who you know you've had a major influence/impact on.

_____

_____

_____

(Now think about how much lives those individuals have changed.)

Describe a time when you didn't think you an impact on a student and you found out later you did.

_____

_____

_____

How do you think your students would describe you as a teacher if they were asked right now?

_____

_____

How do you want your students to remember you as a teacher?

_____

_____

_____

(Consider how alike or how different your past two answers are.)

If you could change one thing about yourself as an educator, what would it be?

_____

_____

_____

What steps are you taking (or can you take) to improve in that one area that you'd like to change.

_____

_____

_____

Who do you know that is an excellent educator?

_____

(Have you told them?)

List qualities that make amazing, life-changing educators.

_____

_____

_____

_____

_____

_____

_____

_____

_____

_____

(How well does this describe you? Keep on striving!)

Never underestimate the power of an educator!

Made in the USA
Columbia, SC
10 June 2025